The Wo
Sutton Hoo

by Jenny Webb
and the children of The Abbey School

First Published in Great Britain in 2001 by
Barny Books

Cover illustration: detail of an Anglo-Saxon brooch by Emma Hamilton

ISBN N° 1 903172 17 9

Published by Barny Books, Hough on the Hill, Grantham, Lincolnshire
Produced by: TUCANN*design&print*, 19 High Street, Heighington Lincoln LN4 1RG
Tel & Fax: 01522 790009
www.tucann.co.uk

In **1939** beneath one of the **barrows*¹** (Mound 1) on **Sutton Hoo,** just outside Woodbridge, archaeologists found the impression of a ship twenty-seven metres long and four metres broad, **clinker built*²** with iron rivets and with **tholes*³** for 14-40 oarsmen. In the middle were traces of a wooden chamber in which it seems a royal person had been laid to rest with a magnificent treasure.

The discovery of this pagan ship burial, thought to be that of **Raedwald,** King of the Eastern Angles and High King of England at that time, opened a window on to the world of the Anglo-Saxons in the C7, shedding brilliant light on a period that had long been known as the **Dark Ages.**

*²clinker built: having a hull constructed with overlapping planks
*³tholes: rowlocks of the ship

THE EARLY ENGLISH
Invasions

The **Romans** invaded Britain in **43 AD** and left in **410AD** when their Empire began to break up. When they left, the remaining population of **Romano-Britons** were largely **christianised.**

There followed three waves of **MIGRATIONS.**
MIGRATION is a movement of people from one place to another.

The first set of **immigrants** in the early Middle Ages were the **Anglo-Saxons.** They were followed by the **Vikings** and finally by the **Normans**.
In each case, the migrants brought armies and took over the land where they wanted to settle. The **time-line** (on page 4) shows when each group invaded.

The **Anglo-Saxons** did not come to Britain in one great invasion. They crossed the sea from Europe in small groups in the fifth and sixth century. After the first invasions by the Anglo-Saxons, many **christianised Britons** moved westwards into Cornwall and Wales or they crossed the sea to Brittany. Their culture was known as **Celtic.**

Although we call these early migrants, **Anglo-Saxons**, they were probably made up of a mixture of tribal groups.
The historian, **Bede**, tells us that they consisted of **Angles** from Denmark, **Saxons** from North Germany and **Jutes** also from Denmark.
Because there is a similarity between the **Old English** language and **Old Frisian**, we now think there were also **Frisians** from North Holland among the migrants.
Archaeologists are now also convinced that **Franks**, migrants from the Frankish Rhineland, now Germany, added to the popu

lation of England, particularly in Kent.

What we call the **Anglo-Saxons**, therefore, were related to the continental **Germanic** tribes and to the **Scandinavians** who, as **Vikings**, later invaded England themselves.

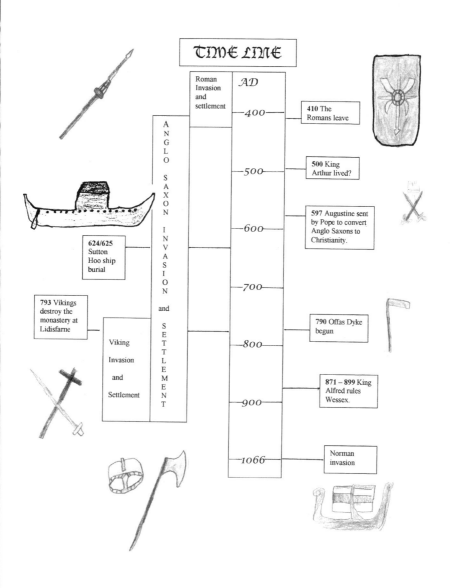

TIME LINE

	Roman Invasion and settlement	AD
		—400— 410 The Romans leave
A N G L O		—500— 500 King Arthur lived?
S A X O N		—600— 597 Augustine sent by Pope to convert Anglo Saxons to Christianity.
624/625 Sutton Hoo ship burial	I N V A S I O N	—700—
793 Vikings destroy the monastery at Lidisfarne	and	790 Offas Dyke begun
Viking Invasion and Settlement	S E T T L E M E N T	—800—
		—900— 871 – 899 King Alfred rules Wessex.
		—1066— Norman invasion

4

WHY DID THEY COME TO SETTLE?

The **Germanic** tribes had been moving south-westwards through Europe for two centuries. The main reason for the migration was the need for more land. With a growing population, farmers were seeking better land for their crops. Some also came because the North Sea had begun to rise and they feared their villages would be flooded.

The first Anglo-Saxons came as warriors. **Bede** writes that when the Romans left in 410AD, the Britons had no defences and were being repeatedly attacked by **Picts** from Scotland.

According to **Bede**, Vortigern, a British ruler, invited the **Angles** and **Saxons** to come to Britain and help fight the **Picts** in return for a promise of land. Twenty years later, they rebelled and over the next fifty years fought the Britons. Gradually they settled down and were joined by other migrants from across the North Sea.

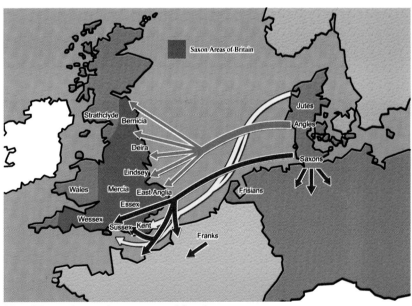

Map of Europe showing the provenance of the tribes.

WHERE DID THEY SETTLE?

The first migrants arrived on the south and east coasts of Britain. The **Jutes** and **Frisians** settled in **Kent,** the **Angles** in **East Anglia** and the **Saxons** in **Wessex.** (See map on page 5)

They cleared more of the forest to make farmland. Family groups joined together and formed settlements. Groups of settlements were ruled by powerful lords who called themselves **kings** after the Old English word for royal family **cyning**.

The land came to be called **England,** from **Angleland**, the land of the **Angles.**

Gradually Anglo-Saxon England was divided into different kingdoms which changed as some got bigger by conquering others. They fought one another for land and power. By 650AD there were seven main kingdoms: **Kent, Northumbria** (Bernicia, Deira and Lindsey)**, Mercia, East Anglia, Sussex, Essex** and **Wessex.** The two biggest kingdoms were **Mercia** and **Northumbria**. Eventually the Kings of **Wessex** became rulers of all England.

There were far fewer settlers in the North and the West and the Anglo-Saxons did not take control of the **Picts** in **Scotland,** the **Scots** in **Ireland** or the **Britons** in **Wales** and **Cornwall.**

Incidentally the origin of the word **Welsh** is Old English and means **foreigner** and **slave**.

Map of Britain, showing the main kingdoms and the Celtic areas.

THE LAND OF
THE EASTERN ANGLES

The land of the **Eastern Angles** was made up of the **North Folk** and the **South Folk**. (The origin of the counties of Norfolk and Suffolk). In the first quarter of the C7, the **Wuffing** King, **Raedwald** was the ruler of the Eastern Angles. **Bede** tells us that his hall was in **Rendlesham**, a few miles from **Sutton Hoo** on the river **Deben** which must have been navigable up to and beyond that point.

Most settlements in Anglo-Saxon England were established within a few miles from a river. **Gyppeswyck**, the Anglo-Saxon name for **Ipswich**, was set up at the mouth of the Orwell and was an important trading settlement from the mid sixth century. (**wic** meant a trading place).

Other sites at **Snape**, **Iken**, **Felixstowe** and **Blythburgh** were similarly placed and emphasise how important the ship was as a means of travel. In those days people travelled on rivers and along the coast as much as possible, it being faster than travelling on horseback. Ships would have travelled from East Anglia to **Canterbury** and also north to **Northumbria** where it was possible to travel quite far inland up many of the big rivers there. It was also a short crossing to ports on the North Sea coast.

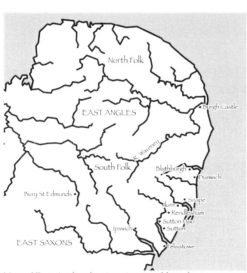

Map of East Anglia showing rivers and key places

THE WUFFINGAS

After years of debate, most archaeologists agree that **Raedwald**, who died in **624/5**, was the man buried in his ship at **Sutton Hoo**. With such a magnificent funeral, the person must have been someone very powerful. Not only had **Raedwald** ruled the Eastern Angles for twenty- five years, he had also been **High King** of England or **Bretwalda**, since 616, a position which, according to **Bede**, allowed him to "hold sway over all the provinces south of the River Humber".

His great-grandfather was **Wehha**, thought to have been the first to rule over the Eastern Angles. His grandfather, **Wuffa**, gave his name to the royal family, the **Wuffingas**, which means **"Little Wolves."**

Raedwald's elder son, **Raegenhere**, was killed at the battle of the **River Idle**, a battle which **Raedwald** successfully fought against **Aethelfrith** of Northumbria in support of **Edwin** who consequently gained the throne. It is through **Bede's** account of this episode that we also gain a strong impression of **Raedwald's wife**, even though we do not know her name.

Bede had already mentioned her in the context of **Raedwald's** conversion to Christianity. According to **Bede**, **Raedwald** kept the altar to the pagan gods in his temple and merely added one to Christ, "seduced by his wife and certain perverse teachers."

He was succeeded by his son **Eorpwald** who converted to Christianity and was killed after only a few years. In 631/2 the kingdom went to his half-brother **Sigebehrt**, a devout Christian, but he preferred the life of a monk and passed the reins of power to **Raedwald's** nephew **Ecric**. When the land was threatened by **Penda** of **Mercia**, **Sigebehrt** was persuaded to leave his monastery and lead his people against **Penda**. According to **Bede** he went into battle armed only with a staff. Both he and **Ecric** were killed and **Anna**, also a Christian, succeeded to the kingdom and ruled until his death in 653.

8

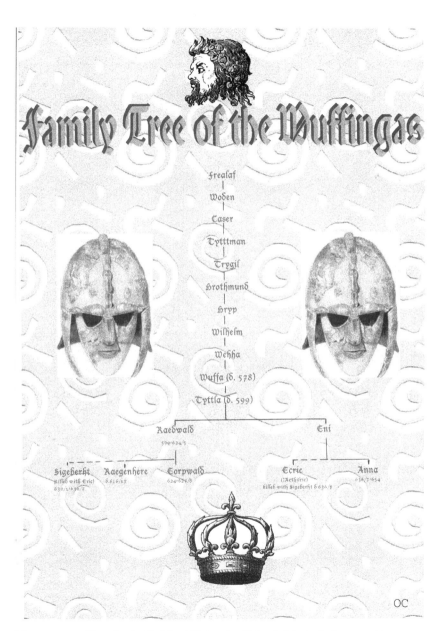

Family Tree of the Wuffingas

Frealaf
|
Woden
|
Caser
|
Tytttman
|
Trygil
|
Hrothmund
|
Hryp
|
Wilhelm
|
Wehha
|
Wuffa (d. 578)
|
Tyttla (d. 599)

Raedwald   Eni
599·624/5

Sigeberht   Raegenhere   Eorpwald   Ecric   Anna
(killed with Eric)   d.616/17   624/627/8   (?Aethric)   636/7·654
630/1/636/7   killed with Sigeberht d 636/7

OC

*Like many pagan kings, **Raedwald** claimed **Woden**, the chief god of the Anglo-Saxons, as his ancestor as if he were a real person. Just as interesting is the fact that he also included **Caesar** in his family tree which shows the continuing strong influence of the Roman Empire.*

9

HOW DO WE KNOW ABOUT THE EASTERN ANGLES?

ARCHEOLOGY: We can learn most about the lives of Anglo-Saxons from archaeology. **Archaeologists** dig up villages and cemeteries. It is possible to identify early Anglo-Saxon settlements through scatters of **pottery sherds***, stray **metalwork finds** and nearby **cemeteries**. The more widespread the area where the sherds are found, the bigger the settlement is believed to be.

Archaeologists have discovered an area north of **St Gregory's Church** in **Rendlesham** which has a extensive pottery scatter. The next large area is in the parish of **Sutton**. So this evidence backs up **Bede's** claim that the seat of the Eastern Angles was in **Rendlesham** four miles from the royal burial ground of **Sutton Hoo**.

Cemeteries provide lots of information about the burial habits of the Anglo-Saxons. Like today there were several methods of burial. Some people were **cremated** and their ashes put in urns. Some were **buried** with their spear or with items of jewellery. Very often a small mound or **barrow** was raised above the burial place to mark the spot where a person of **high status** had been laid to rest. Often they were buried on a piece of high land so that their barrow could be seen from far away.

Ship Burials are associated with the death of kings or chiefs. The most interesting fact is that there have only been **three** ship burials found in England. All three were discovered in **East Anglia**; one was in **Snape** and the other two were found at **Sutton Hoo** which we know to be a royal burial ground.

The only other ship burials have been found in **Scandinavia**, two major sites in **Sweden** at **Vendel** and **Valsgarde** and one in **Norway** in **Oseberg** as well as over 200 other find-spots.

Therefore we think that the royal family of East Anglia, **the**

Wuffingas, may have been related to the **Swedish** royal family and could well be a branch of the **Scylfings** mentioned in "**Beowulf**". (See page 12)

*sherds: bits of broken pottery

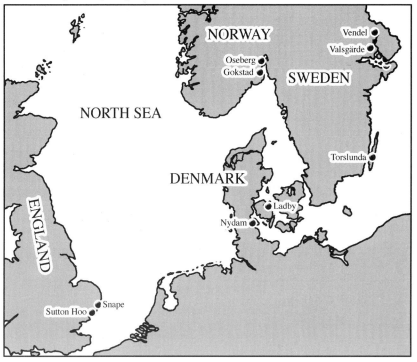

Map showing ship burials in Scandinavia

BEDE: Bede was a monk who lived in **Jarrow** in **Northumbria** in the **C8**. In those times, monks were the only people who could read and write.

In **731** he wrote **"A History of the English Church and People"**. Although he recorded history from a Christian point of view and therefore left out details of some of the pagan kings, he does include useful details about **Raedwald**. He mentioned his hall at **Rendlesham,** describes his conversion to **Christianity** in Kent at the court of **King Aethelbehrt** and records the fact that on his return home he set up a **Christian** altar in his temple alongside the **pagan** one.

BEOWULF: "**Beowulf**" is a long Anglo-Saxon poem which, although set in **Denmark** and **Sweden**, is thought to have been composed and eventually written down in England -possibly **East Anglia** -in the C8.

It tells the story of a monster called **Grendel** who raids the hall of **King Hrothgar** and eats his soldiers. **Beowulf** is the hero from **Geatland** who slays **Grendel** and his mother, the sea-hag, and in later life kills a fire-breathing dragon but is slain in the process.

The anonymous author of the poem describes in detail the life of the hall where the king and the nobles would live. He tells us about the feasting, about the kings who ruled and who kept their nobles loyal by giving them presents of gold. He also describes the magnificent burials given to them. One King, **Scyld Scefing**, was put in his ship with all his treasure and apparently sent out to sea. **Beowulf** himself was cremated and buried along with the dragon's treasure. His funeral mound was built on the headland where it could be seen from far off.

The descriptions of these two funerals with their treasure seem very similar to that of the king buried in his ship at **Sutton Hoo** and makes us wonder whether the original composer of the poem may have witnessed the funeral of **Raedwald.**

THE SHIP

When it was found, the ship had been lying in the damp earth for over 1300 years. The planks of the sides had rotted, leaving a wafer-thin layer, while the 26 massive ribs had completely decayed and been replaced by sand pushed in by the weight of the burial mound above. This meant that a ship exactly like the original could be seen in the ground.

The iron rivets which had held the overlapping planks together, some bolts and even the nails which had fixed a patch in place were all preserved in their original position.

This was the first long ship known in Northern Europe 200 years before the Vikings. The ship had room for 40 oars, 20 on each side, but there is evidence that in this ship, there were no oars in the centre where the royal party would have travelled.

It was steered by a **steering oar** which was attached by a rope on to the right side of the ship. The term **starboard** (steering side) comes from this practice. There was no **keel** but a **keel plank** which made it ideal for navigation in shallow water such as rivers, among sandbanks and creeks.

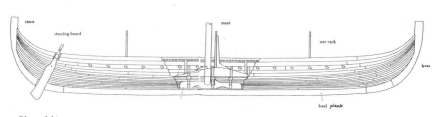

Plan of ship

We do not know whether a **sail** was ever used but a ship of this sort could well have been fitted with one. The middle section was stable and certainly able to carry sail especially in combination with the elegantly shaped **stern** and **bow**. It would certainly have been capable of riding the waves of the channel and the southern part of the North Sea.

HOW WAS THE SHIP BROUGHT UP TO THE HOO?

Although it seems an enormous task to us, pulling ships across land from one water way to another was common practice in those days.

The ship would have been rowed down the Deben from **Rendlesham** and moored at a point on the bank below the burial ground. Then it would have been pulled out of the water and to make it lighter, all its fittings, oars, anchor and rowing benches would have been removed. It would have needed many men to pull it the quarter of a mile up the hill using strong ropes attached to the inside.

Lengths of tree trunks, greased with animal fat would have been pushed under the bows of the ship to act as **skids** or **rollers.**

A great trench, lying east to west, would have been dug before-hand to receive the ship. A cabin with a steeply pitched roof, was built in the centre of the ship, rather like a Noah's ark, to house the King's body and all of his treasure.

After the funeral, the ship and trench were filled in with earth. The roof of the chamber was covered with **turf** and a **circular mound** was raised over the ship to a height of **two and a half metres**. It would have been visible from the river and beyond and as well as being a symbol of the King's power, was also meant to bring prosperous harvests to his people even after his death.

A Cross-section of a Barrow

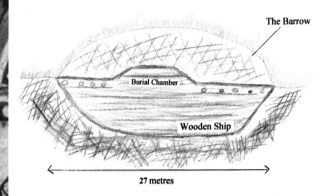

The Barrow

Burial Chamber

Wooden Ship

27 metres

WHY DID HE HAVE A SHIP BURIAL?

The main significance of the ship burial is that it is a **pagan** funeral, not a **Christian** one. Pagans believed that you could travel to the afterlife by ship with all your worldly goods. We know **Raedwald** had been baptised but it is clear that the man buried in his ship was not a committed Christian but a pagan who was looking back to his roots, to his ancestors from Sweden who also had ship burials. The fact that his wife, a strong- minded woman according to Bede, had rejected Christianity must also have influenced the form of the King's funeral.

HOW DID THEY DISCOVER HIS IDENTITY?

The excavators found no trace of a body which at first gave rise to the theory that the grave was a **cenotaph***[1] only. However, where a body would have lain in the centre of the cabin, a concentration of **phosphate***[2] was found. The soil in this particular spot on the hoo is very acid and after nearly 1400 years, it is believed that the bones could well have dissolved in the soil.

There were several clues that helped identify **Raedwald**. The most crucial was a collection of thirty seven gold coins all from different mints in France which dated the burial between 620-625AD. There were also three gold pieces and two little bars of gold. Their number is significant and suggests they could be payment for the 40 ghostly oarsmen and the steersman who would take the ship on its voyage into the next world.

The other clues related to the **grave goods** found in the ship. The graves of **pagans,** especially those of **high status**, were nearly always filled with things that the dead person would need in the after-life. In this grave, the goods were undoubtedly those of a king. They included a huge **whetstone** which was thought to be a royal **sceptre**, an iron **standard,** a **helmet** based on a Roman parade helmet, a great **shield** and **sword** and a **mail**

tunic. The people who buried the King wanted to be sure that when he arrived in the next world, his importance would be recognised. They reflect his role as king, warrior and host.

[1]Cenotaph: monument of commemoration
[2]Phosphate: chemical compound signifying bone deposit

GRAVE GOODS

Signs of Kingship: When the grave was opened, the archaeologists were puzzled by two unusual objects which were found at the head of the grave, signifying that they were of great importance. One was a stone bar with carved faces on it and the other was a long, rusty, iron pole with a cage at the top.

The stone bar is thought to be a **sceptre**, the king's rod of office and a sign of authority. It was made from a **whetstone** of a kind not found in Britain and had four carved faces at either end. There was a red knob at each end and on the bottom, a cage attached to a saucer which could have rested on the king's knee during ceremonies. At the top stood a ring with a bronze stag, a symbol of royalty.

The rusty pole is thought to be a **standard**, another symbol of the king's power and position, to be carried before him in processions as the Romans did. It was probably made locally of iron, measuring nearly **one and three-quarter metres** long and the cage on top had ox heads on it with long curving horns facing inwards. Flags or feathers may have been attached to the cage to flutter in the wind. **Bede** refers to one carried by King Edwin of Northumbria.

Detail of restored sceptre: British Museum

THE KING'S WEAPONS AND ARMOUR

If we look at the weapons and armour found in the Sutton Hoo grave, we can see that they belonged to no ordinary soldier. Most Anglo-Saxon freemen would have only had a **spear** which would have been buried with them when they died but this grave had **nine** spears, three of them barbed, called **angons**. He also had a magnificent **sword** which by itself marked him out as a great leader. In addition he had a decorated **helmet, a coat of chain mail** and a great **shield.**

The **helmet** was based on a **Roman** design. It was made of iron and was padded with leather. At the front was a bronze face mask with a strong nose, a moustached mouth and eyeholes below thick eyebrows. These features were all **gilded** giving the effect of a flying dragon, with red garnets used as eyes. Another dragon head hung from the end of a crest which ran along the top of the helmet. The outer tip of each eyebrow was shaped into a small golden boar's head.

The whole surface was covered in small pictures made of tinned bronze which shone like silver. Some are patterns of twisting snakes, others show scenes of dancing men with horns on their heads, carrying spears.

Another scene is of a horseman trampling a fallen soldier who is stabbing the horse in the chest. (See page 29)

The **shield** was made of limewood and measured almost a **metre** across. Around it was a golden metal rim and the edge was patterned with little gold rectangles and golden dragon heads with red eyes. At the back a hole had been cut out of the wood and a gilded handgrip put in place, shaped like a pair of many-headed dragons. Covering the hole at the front, thereby protecting the man's hand, was a great iron boss covered with gold decorations.

The surface was highly decorated and seems unsuitable for fighting. It may have been used for parades and processions. The ornaments were in the shape of animal heads, an eagle-like bird and a winged dragon. Both **helmet** and **shield** were very similar to those found in **Swedish** graves and could well have been made abroad or by foreign craftsmen working in the royal workshops.

The jewelled **sword** lay by the dead man's side. Not only was it a rich man's weapon, it was also a sign of high rank. To receive one was a mark of high honour and often swords were given names and poems were made up about them.

The sword **blade** was protected by a wooden **scabbard** lined with animal fur to keep the steel well greased so it would stay in good condition. However after hundreds of years in the ground, the blade in the scabbard was a rusty mass and only by using x-rays has it been possible to take a picture of the blade itself and to see that it was of the highest quality. This one was probably made in the **Frankish Rhineland**. The **pommel**[1] sparkled with red garnets set in a pattern of gold. The **hand-guards** across the **hilt**[2] were plates of pure gold.

The **sword belt** must have lain close to the sword. The leather had decayed but the **buckles** and **fittings** did survive and were as richly decorated as the sword itself. All the fittings were of gold with red garnets in a wonderful variety of patterns. Such was the skill of the goldsmith who cut each garnet to fit the gold exactly, that of the 1357 garnets used, only six have come loose or been lost!

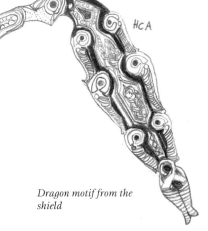

Dragon motif from the shield

[1]Pommel: rounded knob at the end of the hilt
[2]Hilt: handle of sword

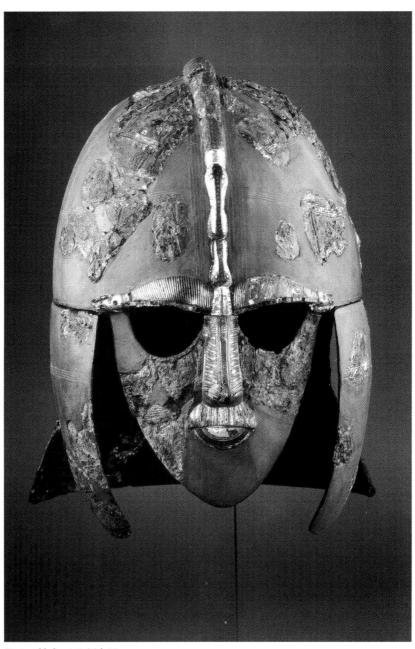

Restored helmet: British Museum

TREASURES

It was obvious to the archaeologists that the man buried in his ship was very rich. He owned some beautiful pieces of jewellery including a heavy **gold buckle**, a **purse lid** made of gold and jewels and a pair of decorated **shoulder clasps** made in the **Roman** style.

The **buckle** is the most valuable piece in the collection, weighing nearly half a kilogram. Although it looks solid, it is hollow and could have been made as a box to hold a small charm. Because there was no trace of cloth or leather with the buckle, we do not know whether it was worn on a belt or hung round the neck on a ribbon.

The top of the buckle is covered with a design of snakes and animals with gaping jaws. They are all so cleverly intertwined that it is hard to distinguish between their legs, jaws and bodies!

The **purse** was made to be hung from a belt held on by straps. The pouch itself had disintegrated being made of leather, but the lid survived.

It had a border of red garnets and panels of coloured glass made into tiny check designs in blue and red or blue and white. This is called **millefiori** and means **"thousand threads"**. There were also pictures fixed to the purse flap also made of garnets and blue and red checked glass. They show a duck held in the claws of an eagle and a man standing between two wolf-like animals.

The **shoulder-clasps** would have fastened his tunic at the shoulders and would have had to be sewn in place. Each clasp was made in two pieces so that half could be sewn to the front of the tunic and half to the back. The two halves were held together by a gold pin hanging on a gold chain. The top of each pin is made in the shape of a tiny boar's head and there are boars too in the design on the clasps themselves. The whole surface is covered in patterns and animal designs. Together with the gold and the sparkling stones, they make a stunning ornament.

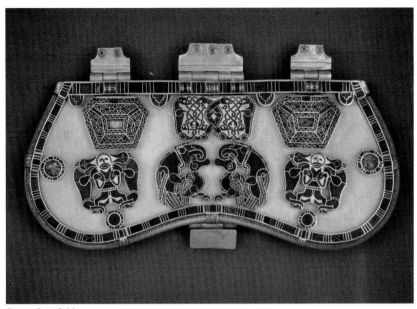

Purse: British Museum

Buckle: British Museum

As well as being a King and a warrior, Raedwald was also a good host. In **"Beowulf"**, the poet describes the life of the hall in great detail. There would be great feasting and storytelling in the evenings and there the King would reward his followers with gold. There are many items in the Sutton Hoo grave which reflect this aspect of Anglo-Saxon life.

There were many drinking vessels, including a magnificent pair of **drinking horns**, made from the **auroch**, a species of cattle, now extinct. They were **60cm** (24ins) long and were decorated with beautiful gold fittings modelled on to the top and bottom. In addition there were six maple wood bottles decorated with silver-gilt mounts and seven small walnut cups also with silver rims.

NH

There were many **silver vessels** also, Two, however, were very large and came from the **Roman** world. One was **fluted** and measured **40cm** (16 ins) across. It had two handles and was decorated with a classical head. When it was dug up, it contained a number of combs and other personal items. The second silver vessel is known as the **Anastasius Dish**, with stamps on its base showing it was made in the **Byzantine Empire**, present- day Turkey, during the reign of **Anastatius 1** (491-518). It measured just over **71cm** across (28 ins) and burnt bone was found on it suggesting a last meal was placed on it for the King. Another unusual vessel was a bronze bowl from Egypt known as the **Coptic** bowl.

Other **domestic vessels** included three huge bronze **cauldrons**, one with a long, ornate **suspension chain** measuring nearly **4.5 metres** (11 feet) which shows it must have been suspended from a cross beam of **5 metres** over the fire. Wooden vessels were also found, a big tub and three smaller buckets of yew bound with iron and having decorated handles.

H.J

The pre-Christian Anglo-Saxons could not read or write and therefore there was a strong **oral** tradition . The poet's memories were the people's libraries and accompanied by his **lyre**, he would entertain the King and his thegns with stories of their ancestors, tales of bravery and fighting.

The **lyre** found in the grave at Sutton Hoo was a six stringed instrument, like a harp and was made of maple wood. It had been put in a beaverskin bag. Near the top of the lyre were metal figures of birds of prey. There was also a set of **ivory gaming pieces**, showing that the Anglo-Saxons loved to gamble.

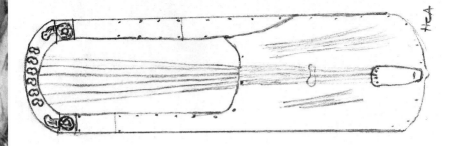

There was strong evidence that the King, though opting for a **pagan** funeral had come into contact with the **Christian** world. A pair of silver spoons of the **Roman** type, some **25cm** (ten ins) long were found in the grave and on their handles are inscribed in Greek letters the words **Saulus** and **Paulus.** It is thought they could have been a christening present. A set of ten small silver bowls measuring **23cm** (9 ins) in diameter each with a **cruciform motif** on its base could also have been a gift or been acquired through trade.

Three bronze hanging bowls of **Celtic** origin were found, one with a fish rising from a pedestal inside it. The fish is a Christian symbol and this one could be rotated by the finger. All the bowls were decorated with enamelled **escutcheons*** on the outside and the largest bowl had been patched with a piece of silver from the Sutton Hoo workshops, stamped with a fierce bird head.

Other interesting items were a little iron lamp which was perhaps lit just before the King was boarded up in his cabin. A tiny bronze bell was also found which suggests that perhaps a favourite pet was buried with him.

Practical items included a set of clothes, leather shoes, otter skin cap, woven cloaks and other textiles. The excavators even found a ladybird and the remains of blue flower.

*Escutcheon: a shield

TRADE

In England at this time, the normal way of paying for things was by exchange of goods. This was called **barter**. The earliest known English coins were not made until twenty-five years after the Sutton Hoo burial.

Across the Channel in France, **barter** was also the most common method of trading but money was made there earlier than in England.

All the **37** coins found in the grave at Sutton Hoo were from France ruled by **Merovingian** kings. They were all from different **mints** from different parts of the country, the furthest being from **Arles** in the South of France. Each mint used its own stamps to mark the coins with signs or portrait heads and the weight of gold was very carefully controlled.

Although many of the grave goods found at Sutton Hoo must have been made in local workshops, many others were **imports** from all over the known world and reveal the extent of trade in the C7.

The English **exported** such goods as wool, grain, cowhides and slaves. They **imported** furs, walrus hide, wood tar (from conifers), swords, mill stones of basalt lava from Northern Europe, textiles, bronze bowls, glass ware and wine from the Mediterranean and precious stones, gold and ivory from the Middle East.

All the raw materials for making jewellery had to be **imported.** Some of the most beautiful of the Sutton Hoo jewellery such as the shoulder clasps and the purse were made of **gold, blue amethysts** and **red garnets. Garnets** came from India and Ceylon and **amethysts** from India or the Eastern Mediterranean.

The **gold** was formerly obtained from the **East Roman** empire but it became harder to come by and craftsmen had to melt down imported coins for their ornaments or add silver to it.

Other items in the ship grave which give an idea of the extent of the trading routes were a heavy bronze bowl made in **Egypt** and silver dishes, bowls and spoons from the empire of **Byzantium** where **Turkey** now stands. These may have been gifts or may have arrived through trade.

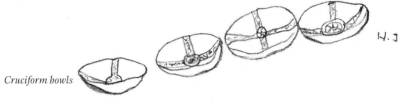

Cruciform bowls

TRADE ROUTES

You can see from the map which trade routes, both by sea and overland, were regularly used:

• *Overland to the Celtic lands in the West and across the Irish Sea.*

• *Trading with Scandinavia across the North Sea. The sea route to Frisia was hardly longer than that to London.*

• *Crossing the North Sea to the Frankish Rhineland, travelling through the Rhine valley down to Italy and beyond the Adriatic to the East Mediterranean, Alexandria and Byzantium (now Istanbul in Turkey).*

• *Crossing the Channel from Kent to France from where many luxury goods, such as glass bottles and jugs and wine were traded. Travelling down through France by road or river, it was also possible to obtain goods from Egypt and the Middle East from other traders.*

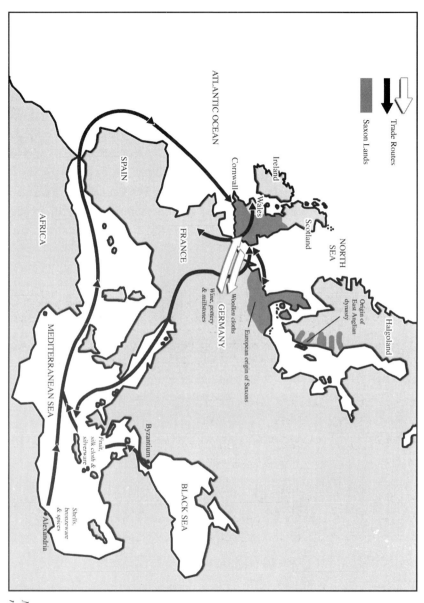

Map showing trade routes

The languages and traditions of all the peoples who made up the **Anglo-Saxons**, were similar in many ways. Before the arrival of **Christianity** in **597** with **Augustine**, they were **pagans** worshipping many gods. There is no written record of paganism except in travellers' tales such as those written by the Roman **Tacitus** in his "**Germania**" and in Scandinavian mythology.

The four main Anglo-Saxon gods were **Woden, Frig, Thunor** and **Tiw**. Even today their influence can be seen in the names of the days of the week. (Compare these with the French who used the Roman gods.)

Days of the Week

E N G L I S H	Monday	Tuesday	Wednesday	Thursday	Friday
	Moon Day	Tiw's Day	Woden's Day	Thunor's Day	Frig's Day
F R E N C H	Lundi	Mardi	Mercredi	Jeudi	Vendredi
	Lune Day	Mars' Day	Mercury's Day	Jove's Day	Venus' Day

Woden was the chief god of the Anglo-Saxons and can be compared with the Norse sky god **Odin**. He was popular with warriors and rulers many of whom, including Raedwald, claimed him as their ancestor.

Woden's influence is seen in many of the grave goods at Sutton Hoo. He was supposed to have power over animals like **snakes**. The snake motif is very popular in Anglo-Saxon jewellery as seen in the great gold buckle found at Sutton Hoo which is made up of nineteen intertwining serpents.

He had two **ravens** as **familiars** and cruel birds of prey feature on much of the metal work found in the burial such as on the **lyre**, the **shield** and the **purse** where a gold and garnet bird of prey catches a duck (See page 21).

Woden was also god of battles and the slain. He chose who was to be slain. On one of the plaques from the Sutton Hoo helmet there is a fallen warrior being trampled by a horse which he stabs with his sword. A tiny figure on the horse guides the spear of the rider. He could be one of Woden's agents, the Valkyries. Another plaque on the helmet is of dancing warriors, men wearing horned helmets dancing and carrying spears.

Frig was Woden's wife and was the goddess of love and fertility, like the Roman goddess, **Venus**. Germanic people in general seem to have respected the wisdom of women. **Frig** may also have been identified with Mother Earth whose favour was essential if the tribe were to survive. She had her festival at the pagan new year on 25 December, **Mother's Night**. Two other goddesses mentioned by **Bede** are **Hrede** and **Eostre**, goddesses of the east and the dawn who were celebrated in March and April. (**Eostre** gives us our name for Easter.)

Her equivalent in Scandinavian mythology was **Freyja** who had a twin brother **Freyr**. Both these gods were associated with **boars** which usually appear in Anglo-Saxon culture as protective symbols for warriors.

Gilded boars can be found on the cheek pieces of the Sutton Hoo helmet.

Also interlaced boars of gold and garnet decorate the royal shoulder clasps found at Sutton Hoo. Lastly there is a boar figure on one of the Christian hanging bowls found in the ship burial.

Thunor was a son of Woden and was associated with thunder. He is the equivalent of the Roman god **Jove** or **Jupiter**. Like the Scandinavian god **Thor**, he carried a short handled hammer. His symbol was the swastika which perhaps represents the lightning which he created. This symbol has been found on Anglian **cremation urns**, and **amulets** made in the shape of a hammer have been found in women's graves.

There is a story told about **Thunor** which involves a fight between him and a giant armed with a **whetstone** (used for sharpening metal tools and weapons.) A piece of the whetstone lodged in Thunor's head and perhaps explains why he is associated with power over lightning and fire since a whetstone sharpens and causes sparks! The sceptre found at Sutton Hoo was a decorated whetstone which was a symbol of the power of the King.

Tiw was the god of battle like the Roman god, **Mars**, and Tuesday was named after him. He was probably the chief god before Woden took over his role. He may have been associated with sacred horses which played a part in northern religions.

The horse appears on the boss of the Sutton Hoo shield and a similar design of interlacing horses is worked in garnet cloisons on the purse lid. The arrow rune represented the name of Tiw and was traditionally carved on weapons to ensure victory.

Thus, the Sutton Hoo ship burial can be seen as the last gasp of paganism in England. Just twenty-five years after the death of Raedwald, the whole of the country had largely been christianised.

However, as this small book has sought to show, the world of Sutton Hoo was not a narrow, pagan one but a rich mixture of diverse influences, including that of the Romans, the Scandinavians and the emerging Christian culture. Far from being a dark age, it was one which had contacts with the whole of the known world and showed levels of craftsmanship and skilled seamanship that anticipate the age of the Vikings.

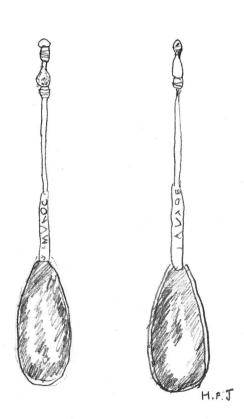

A SELECTIVE BIBLIOGRAPHY

FOR CHILDREN

Katherine East: *A King's Treasure-The Sutton Hoo Ship Burial:* Kestrel 1982
Margaret Sharman: *Anglo-Saxons:* Evans Bros 1995
Martyn Whittock: *Living in Anglo-Saxon England:* Heinemann 1996
Kings, Chiefs and Warriors: Heinemann 1996
Beliefs and Myths of Anglo-Saxon England: Heinemann 1997
Robert Hull: *The Anglo-Saxons:* Heritage 1997
Rosemary Sutcliffe: *Dragon Slayer:* Red Fox 1992
John Reeve and Jenny Chattington: *The Anglo-Saxon Activity Book* : British Museum 1996
Jenny Webb: *Farewell the King: A Tale of Sutton Hoo:* Barny Books 2000

FOR ADULTS

Angela Care Evans: *The Sutton Hoo Ship Burial:* British Museum Press 1992
Martin Carver: *Sutton Hoo: Burial Ground of Kings?*: British Museum Press 1998
Kathleen Herbert: *Looking for the Lost Gods of England:* Anglo-Saxon Books 1994
Gale Owen: *Rites and Religion of the Anglo-Saxons:* Barnes and Noble 1996
Martin Welch: *Anglo-Saxon England:* English Heritage Book Batsford 1992
Ed. James Campbell: *The Anglo-Saxons:* Penguin 1991